NELLIE BLY
Reports the News

by **Tekla White**
illustrated by **Carolyn Vibbert**

MODERN CURRICULUM PRESS
Pearson Learning Group

Nelly Bly

Stephen Collins Foster

Nel-ly   Bly! – Nel-ly Bly! bring the broom a - long. We'll sweep the kitch-en

clean, my dear and love a little song.   Poke the wood, my lady love. And

In 1885, a young woman named Elizabeth Cochran moved to Pittsburgh, Pennsylvania, with her mother. She wanted to work to earn money for her family. But there weren't many good jobs for women at that time.

One day Elizabeth saw a story in a local newspaper, the *Pittsburgh Dispatch*. And what she read made her very angry. The writer thought women shouldn't work away from home as men did. Elizabeth wrote a letter to the newspaper. She said that women could do many kinds of work just as well as men. The problem was that no one offered women jobs with good pay.

Her correspondence with the editors led to a job at the *Dispatch*. She decided to use a different name when she became a reporter. She chose Nellie Bly—a name from a popular song.

Bly went to factories and wrote about the lives of workers. She learned that women in bottle factories were often injured in accidents. The factories were so cold in the winter that women wrapped their feet in rags to keep warm. They worked long hours without rest.

Many workers came from foreign countries. Their pay was very low. They couldn't pay much rent. Bly wanted to know where a foreigner could find a place to live. She found that many lived in buildings that weren't clean or safe.

Because of Bly's articles, the *Dispatch* sold many newspapers. People bought the *Dispatch* just to read Bly's stories.

The factory owners and landlords were angry. They didn't want Nellie Bly to write stories about them. If she didn't stop, they said they wouldn't pay to advertise in the newspaper. The newspaper needed the money from advertisements, so the editors at the *Dispatch* told Bly to write only about things that wouldn't make anyone angry.

The editor sent Bly to see a nice new jail. She thought the new jail was better than the old ones. But she didn't write much about the new jail. Instead she wrote about the old dirty jails. Bly's readers then wanted the old jails improved. That made the city leaders angry. They didn't have enough money to improve all the jails.

The editors also sent Bly to Mexico. She wanted to write about the Mexican people. The editors felt it was too dangerous for a woman to travel by herself. But she didn't give up. She told the editors she would vacation in Mexico. They could print her correspondence if they liked what she wrote.

Bly wrote about places and people in Mexico. She sent her stories to the *Dispatch*. They were printed by newspapers all over the United States.

Bly also wrote about the Mexican government. Some Mexican leaders who saw the stories didn't like the fact that a foreigner was writing about their country. They threatened her. She knew it was time to go home.

Some friends told Bly to hide the rest of her stories. That was because agents could put her in jail if they didn't like what she wrote. Bly packed her stories with her clothes. Luckily, the agent at the border didn't search her clothing. He helped Bly board the train for home.

Other newspapers wanted Bly as a reporter. Bly traveled to New York City. There, she began to write for the *New York World*. Her articles were very popular. She was one of the first reporters to go undercover. Bly would pretend that she was not a reporter. She would pretend to be like the people she was writing about. This way she was able to find out things that people would never have told her if they knew she was writing an article.

Bly was concerned about the way certain groups of people were treated. She was especially concerned about the treatment of women and the poor. They were often ignored. Nellie was able to help these people by writing articles about them.

For example, once she went undercover as a servant. Then she wrote about the poor conditions in which servants lived. People who read her article were shocked. They saw a side of the world that they did not know. Some also demanded better treatment of servants.

Bly continued to write for the *New York World*. She wrote about factories, politicians, and the police. The *World* sold more and more newspapers. People wanted to read what Nellie Bly thought about their city. When people met the young reporter, they often expressed their gratitude for her stories.

One day, Bly read Jules Verne's popular book, *Around the World in Eighty Days*. She thought she could travel faster than Phileas Fogg, the character in Verne's book. She asked the editors at the newspaper to send her around the world. The editors liked the idea, but they decided to send a man instead. They felt that women shouldn't travel alone in other countries.

Bly argued with her editors until they agreed she could go. She left New Jersey by ship on November 14, 1889. Eight days later, Bly arrived in London, England.

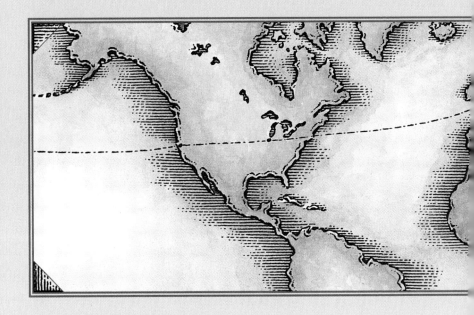

Bly visited the author, Jules Verne, in France. He wished her luck. He didn't think she could travel around the world in fewer than eighty days.

After a ride on a mail train to Italy, Nellie boarded a ship for Egypt and then Ceylon. But the boat to Singapore left two days late. Her trip was delayed even longer in Singapore.

To pass time, Bly took a trip to China. She went shopping for exotic souvenirs. She bought a lively, short-tailed monkey. Bly and her exotic pet took a steamship to Hong Kong and then went on to the United States.

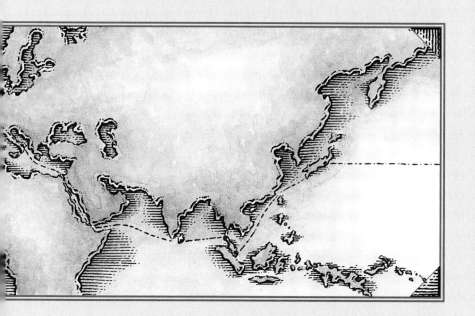

Soon Bly learned that another writer wanted to beat her record. The other writer was going around the world in the opposite direction. And she was making better time.

In San Francisco, huge crowds came to see Nellie Bly. Blizzards kept trains from traveling the shortest way across the country. There wasn't much time left. Even if Bly reached New Jersey in fewer than eighty days, the other writer might get there first.

But in the end, Bly won the race. Bly's train arrived in Jersey City at 3:51 P.M. on January 25, 1890. Her 24,899-mile journey took seventy-two days, six hours, and eleven minutes. The other writer didn't arrive until four days later. Nellie Bly's globe-circling record held until 1929.

Nellie Bly spent most of her life trying to help people. At one point she bought and managed her own factories. These factories made such things as metal containers. The people who worked for her enjoyed good working conditions and pay.

But after a while, her business did not go well. She had to close the factories. Nellie decided to travel to Europe for a vacation. World War I began. She would not go back to the United States until the war was over.

When Nellie returned to New York City, she wrote about homeless children who were living on city streets. People read her stories and helped these children. Nellie also found homes for many orphans. She wrote in order to make life better for people.

Nellie Bly died on January 27, 1922.

She had earned the gratitude of workers and poor people throughout the United States.